LEAD WITH GRACE: LEADING COMMUNITY IN DISRUPTIVE TIMES

****

This is

THE SHEPHERD METAPHOR

Dr VICKY MCGAHEY

First published 2018 by

Vicky McGahey

www.vickymcgahey.com

© Vicky McGahey

FREE POSTER

Vicky has written a verse on GRACE
which is shared with you in the opening pages
of this book.

Get your FREE Copy of selected prose below…

Grace is not seen,
but felt

Often not spoken,
but is heard in the
silence

Get My FREE Poster

For

Those who search within
themselves
for happiness and peace
AND
My Mum

Email: vicky@vickymcgahey.com
Website: vickymcahey.com
**Available for Keynote Presentations
and Workshops**

FREE WORK BOOK

Get your <u>FREE</u> **WORK BOOK** to record your thoughts and reflections.

It includes mandalas to colour in. The work book is designed to accompany the book

Leadership Attributes for Women and Men: Leading Community in Disruptive Times

Visit my website for other FREE resources

<u>www.vickymcgahey.com</u>

Also available at the website is other helpful resources including **The Leadership Attributes Game**.

CONTACT EMAIL:
<u>vicky@vickymcgahey.com</u>

Available for Keynote Presentations and Workshops

Table of Contents

About the Author

"I am a teacher, speaker and author. I help people realise their potential to lead and find their voice so as they create life-giving communities within the home, workplace and the world. I also love to restore old fountain pens and sing."

Vicky McGahey was born in Perth, Western Australia. She has lived in Sydney for most of her life and has worked as a teacher, entertainer, speaker and lecturer. Vicky has a doctorate degree and several masters degrees, including one in Theology. Her doctorate focused on the subject of leadership and the attributes required to be a good and moral leader. Vicky is a high school teacher of religion, science and music. She has held several head teacher roles including Director of Human Resources. Vicky is an a Past President of Rotary who was award a Paul Harris Fellowship for leadership.

Vicky is also the author of a children's fantasy and science fiction series titled The Kingdom of Wizards. The series features fantasy stories, each founded in reality and filled with mystery and adventure. The stories teach the young mind that the ability to lead lies within us all - which makes it a good read for all ages.

Vicky is an accomplished singer and a songwriter who is a keynote speaker and presenter. As an active member of the community, her interests include politics, leadership theory and practice, theology, the Australian bush, scuba diving, self-reflection, writing and the study of the voice.

Vicky is continuing her studies and work around the topic of 'women who lead.' She believes the voice of women should be heard in determining vision, mission and direction of organisations no matter what position they hold - executive to canteen lady.

FORWARD

We have been back and forth, in and out, through the inevitable maze of chaos that is 'the ways of doing leadership.' Moreover, we have yet to touch the soul of leadership and released its essence. This essence is found within all of us and it emerges we sense the spirit, a spirit within. When we open ourselves to listen, we can begin to sense that who we are now and the who we can be, is already within us. I believe we need 'grace' to release it.

Also, we need people of grace to lead us - women and men.

We need leaders to become engaged in a 'spirit of service' that informs and directs their actions as leaders of a community. In doing so, they lead with grace. However, to do this effectively, leaders must discover and uncover specific attributes (qualities) within themselves. A study on leadership and leadership attributes revealed the key attributes leaders need to develop within themselves to help create community - in particular, a moral community (McGahey, 2000c). From this study, a strategy has been designed to reveal the leadership attributes required of a leader in various scenarios. The strategy is called the Leadership Attributes Game (LAG). A full description of the game is beyond the scope of this essay. The book Leadership Attributes for Women and Men: Leading Community in Disruptive Times. Visit my website for details of the book and game at www.vickymcgahey.com.

The Leadership Attributes form part of the Shepherd Metaphor of Leadership which along with the concept of to lead with grace are the two main subjects of this book. The plight of women in leadership and the lack thereof in work and community life is shameful.

The concept of 'Leading with Grace' was first discussed within the realm of leadership in two refereed papers presented by me several years ago. Each titled 'Leading With Grace' McGahey (2012) and McGahey (2013) - see reference list at the end of this book for details. In more recent times the notion of leading with grace has become a popular subject.

Sincerely, to gather people together, a leader needs to create a vision of a possible future and then develop a mission. A vision and mission should always herald a call to action. To lead with grace is a call to action even if that may mean no action. Without a doubt, to lead with grace is an act of service. It begins through the conscious and willing act of listening...and to be still!

So be still as you read. Good luck with that!

INTRODUCTION
Simplicity

Simplicity is one of the hardest constructs to grasp, produce and maintain in any human endeavour and so it is when writing on leadership. The simplicity of explanation is lost when its execution is reliant on human action. Leadership is more than a concept it is a subject for it lies at the heart of thought and action in the formation of communities within family, groups and organisations.

Simplicity is a paradox when we think of the complexity of our lives. Many solutions and answers to problems are found in the simplicity of a few words, a simple good deed or simply the gift of time we give to ourselves in contemplation and to others.

Edward Debono wrote a book called 'simplicity, were he described 'the human minds way of simplifying the world around us' was through the use of concept(s). Debono, 1998, p. 284).

Grace is a simple concept and leadership is a multifaceted concept. To lead with grace is a complex task. How can we bring 'grace' and 'leadership' together. How can we make it simple and achievable?

One answer is through the use of metaphor. A metaphor is a symbolic representation that can be used to develop an understanding of the qualities and values unpinning a concept(s). It is also useful when trying to describe the interactions between different concepts.

The Shepherd Metaphor for Leadership as given in this book is an insightful way towards building community through grace filled leadership. The visual metaphor is simplistic but the commentary to support its thesis displays the complexity of leaders work and leadership per se. The metaphor evolved through research, reflection and an extensive review of relevant literature.

The Shepherd Metaphor is an instrument that encourages a 'way of being' that we should seek within ourselves as we live our daily life. More importantly, it lies at the heart of the catchphrase for leading with grace - 'a graceful vision for a grace-filled mission is a call to action.' That action can be in the service of others. However, the catch cry is more than that, it is a war cry!

Moreover, as such, it has purpose, direction and action. Along with The Shepherd Metaphor, it creates and sustains presence through the shared vision, mission and actions of individuals who chose to form communities that are inherently moral. The establishment of authentic relationships built upon trust is a feature of such communities. Whether or not those communities are found in business, organisations, charities or indeed, a family.

This book will first define grace in the simplest of terms and the idea of leading with grace. To 'lead with grace' will be described and examples of past and present leaders who led with grace. They were blessed with a graceful vision successfully executed through the actions of a grace-filled mission. The book _Leadership Attributes for Women and Men: Leading Community in Disruptive Times_ tells of their stories. The stories evoke a 'sense of the spirit' of what it is to lead with grace.

The Shepherd Leadership Metaphor which includes the Leadership Attributes acts as a guide for those who seek to establish community. The attributes are the qualities that every person can develop within themselves whether they aspire to lead or not.

Chapter 1
GRACE

Grace is not seen but is felt.
Often not spoken, but is heard in the
silence.
Not always found in some act, but
through inaction.
Divine but also human - a gift we can
pass onto others.

Grace is all around me as you are at the
centre of my thoughts.
It is both a presence and a place.
It is a connection to something bigger
than ourselves.

Grace seeks wisdom and wisdom seeks
grace.
Grace can be found in a great temple as
well as in a grain of sand.
On the breath of the wind and in the
charism of a good person.

Grace is life-giving, it calls us to serve.
Grace is in the present, past and future
as it will be in the end.
Grace is but a moment in time.

Grace lives within us -
In all of us.

(McGahey, 2012)

Grace is a powerful word. However, it can evoke within us a sense of softness and calmness. The poem is an attempt to present some of the mystery, purpose and meaning to the word 'grace'. These are the first words I wrote in contemplation upon grace.

Grace is seen in action as a form of movement or a simple act - usually one of kindness, graciousness and generosity. The meaning of grace has historical and cultural significance. It is as full of complexity as it is simple.

A brief definition of grace from a religious perspective is described below to sense the place of grace within a secular, pluralistic and global world.

'Words cannot define grace; it motion and action.' (Casey Kochmer, 2012)

Traditionally grace has been associated with womanhood rather than manhood. To be graceful is a quality usually attributed to a woman. However, modernity has challenged this belief with a 'crossover' and a blending of the sexes where the new age bloke has come of age. Many leaders are finding the grace-filled side of leadership does reap rewards of loyalty, respect and long-lasting relationships that mean you are not alone - you have followers; you have a tribe.

The word grace can mean many things. It is used to describe the attributes (qualities) of a person. Like for example, a disposition to kindness and compassion, and a pleasing or charming quality. A person maybe grace-filled and seen to be gracious. It can be said of such a person 'How gracious you are.' Grace is an ideal that we strive to reach (McGahey, 2012).

The religious and spiritual perspective of grace is of particular significance for many religions. Grace can be used to describe a state of being and a spiritual presence. Grace is said to be a gift from God as given in 1 Peter 5-10: 'God opposes the proud, but gives grace to the humble.' It can be an act of goodwill. The song Amazing Grace stirs the heart and soul of people when played or sung.

The word grace is used to describe an object or a piece of art when expressed as elegance and beauty of movement, form, expression, or proportion. In Greek and Roman mythology grace is associated with three sister goddesses known as Aglaia, Euphrosyne, and Thalia. The sisters dispense charm and beauty to those who sought it (Kren and Marx, 2012).

(National Galleries, 2012)

The picture depicts the neoclassic sculpture by Antonio Canova (1814 – 1817) of the three sisters. The 6th Duke of Bedford commissioned the work, and it is on display in the Victoria and Albert Museum or the National Galleries of Scotland.

It takes time to develop grace in movement, song and any expression of beauty. It requires patience, eloquence and confidence with a dash of quiet humility.

For this book, it suffices to describe the profound nature of grace as given in the verse above. Grace manifests itself in the human qualities/attributes, actions that are gracious, graceful and grace-filled. Many of these are found in the Shepherd Metaphor for Leadership, one of the subjects of this book. The metaphor speaks of a call to action in the service of others. A graceful vision for a grace-filled mission of an organisation or community should herald a call to action.

The other subject of this book is to lead with Grace with Grace. I pose the questions:

1. Why lead with Grace.

2. What is like to lead with Grace.

Chapter 2
LEAD WITH GRACE

Warren Bennis is a leadership theory pioneer and guru now in his nineties. During an interview, Bennis said he was not religious however, his next book would be on the importance of grace. It would include discussion around the concepts of 'generosity, respect, redemption and sacrifices. All of which sound vaguely spiritual, but all of which, I think are going to be required for leadership.' (Bennis, 2010). Bennis hinted at the spiritual nature of leadership which is a concept not uncommon in recent literature and the myriad of courses offered in universities, colleges and online (Australian Catholic University and Harvard University to mention a few) (McGahey, 2012).

Her Royal Highness Queen Elizabeth II is a current world leader who is asking people to search deep within themselves to find innate goodness. In her Jubilee speech to parliament during 2012, she spoke of the need for people to grow in resilience, tolerance and ingenuity (Elizabeth II, R, 2012). Mary Robinson, past President of Ireland and United Nations ambassador, while visiting Australia spoke about world poverty. She cited the United Nations as stressing the need for peoples and corporations to develop integrity, transparency and accountability in what they do (Big Ideas, ABC, 2009).

The qualities or 'ideals' of generosity, respect, resilience, tolerance, ingenuity, integrity, transparency, accountability (responsibility) and with the addition of authenticity (Bezzina, Burford & Duignan, 2007; McGahey, 2002; Starratt, 2005) can be fostered in practices through the attributes and actions of a leader as given in the Shepherd Metaphor. In this way, grace-filled and authentic relationships are built and nurtured. Several writers in the field of leadership have realised the significance of relationships (personal and group) in organisations and the formation of communities (Bezzina, 2012; Bowling, 2011; McGahey, 2000, 2002; Sergiovanni, 1996; Starratt, 2012). The Shepherd Metaphor is a way to help leaders lead with grace.

To lead with grace is described by Dean James Ryan of Harvard University in his 2017 Commencement address to students.

'To lead with grace, to me means to lead with gratitude and with courage. It means to lead with forgiveness and to lead in the service of others. It means to lead with authenticity and with a combination of confidence and humility.'

There are many leaders past and present whose actions have mirrored a person who leads with grace. An example of a leader displaying this is Abraham Lincoln. Lincoln is well known for his belief in keeping friends close and your enemies closer (Goodwin, 2009). This practice was first attributed to Sun-Tzu, a Chinese general and military strategist in the 400BC (The Art of War). Lincoln worked hard to ensure everyone understood his intentions and he understood theirs. He strived to forge meaningful and productive relationships with those around him. From this position hopefully, one can create new and better realities that are beneficial to everyone.

Another notable leader with grace is Mahatma Gandhi. Gandhi would not ask of others what he was not prepared to do. He often said 'You must become the change you wish to see in the world.' One of the stories that personified Gandhi's words is about a mother and child who came to visit him. At a large gathering convened so that Gandhi could address the people, a mother seized the opportunity to have the great sage teach her son a lesson. The little boy was extremely partial to sugar. The following is a scripted version of the event.

The mother asked Gandhi to tell the boy that too much sugar was not good for his teeth and his diet.
Gandhi looked at the child and his mother, then harshly replied, 'I cannot tell him that!'

He proceeded to walk away. After a moment's reflection, he turned and said, 'But you may bring him back in one month's time.'

The woman was frustrated, as she thought Gandhi would support her in her efforts to ensure her child ate wisely. Nonetheless, in a month's time she returned with her son, not knowing what to expect. They had travelled some distance on both occasions. Upon seeing them, Gandhi knew exactly who they were. He knelt down and beckoned the child to him. Gracefully, he smiled at the boy and wisely he said, 'Do not eat sugar! It is not good for you!' Gandhi hugged the child and passed him back to his mother.

The mother was grateful but asked, 'Why did you not tell my son this weeks ago?' Gandhi sighed and replied, 'Four weeks ago I was still eating sugar!'

(McGahey, 2018; Lee, 1997)

Gandhi would not ask of others what he was not prepared to do. As he always said, 'Asked only what you would do.'

And so it was, that the simplest of acts had a profound impact upon Gandhi and those around him.

The power of integrity is found in the simplicity of truth.

Abraham Lincoln, Mahatma Gandhi, Queen Elizabeth II, Malala Yousafzai, Saint Mary Mackillop of The Cross (first and only Australian Saint), Mother Therese of Calcutta, Benjamin Franklin, Eleanor Roosevelt, Dalai Lama, Dr Martin Luther King and other leaders have been people who lead with grace. *The book Leadership Attributes for Women and Men: Leading Community in Disruptive Times* has many stories of leaders who lead with grace.

To lead with grace is as complex as it is simple. It is not easily defined in words but can be eloquently described through story. Such are the paradoxes of life.

To lead with grace is to seek to build authentic relationships of trust in the formation of community (McGahey, 2012). Even relationships with those whom you do not like. This can be achieved through the living of leadership attributes and actions as given in the Shepherd Metaphor that encourages authentic relationships of trust and the formation of community (McGahey, 2013).

Chapter 3
THE SHEPHERD METAPHOR

The purpose of the Shepherd Metaphor for Leadership is the establishment of communities that are inherently moral within organisations, families and groups. This is achieved through the building of authentic and trusting relationships were the emphasis is on people rather than roles. There are many scholarly definitions of a moral community. For this book, a simple definition of is:

'A community that is built upon shared values, norms and beliefs, and one that values the heart, soul and mind of its people.' (McGahey, 2001, p. 37)

Images and metaphors can be used to explain and develop an understanding of qualities and associated values (Laniak, 2006; Sergiovanni 1992; Spicer, 2011). Sergiovanni (1992, p. 45), when speaking of common norms, values and beliefs as being the essence of moral leadership states 'they frame the way we think about management, leading and schooling, and they create the reality that we ultimately live.'

The Christian image of Jesus of Nazareth is a possible exemplar for the context of building a moral community. The Bible refers to Jesus as the Good Shepherd who displayed the characteristics of a caring, loving, influential leader of the flock. However, one should not restrict the image of a shepherd to a Christian perspective. Shepherds have been associated with Christian and non-Christian cultures (Lamiak, 2006). Pictures and paintings of shepherds past depict the role of herding as being shared amongst the sexes. Women, men and children are drawn traversing fields of green with a crook in hand as they tend their flock (Carnes, 2007; McGahey, 2000).

Figure 1 is a visual display of the Shepherd Metaphor for Leadership. It consists of several key features: The Guiding Principle; The Attributes of a Shepherd; and the Shepherd Actions. An essential concept of the Shepherd Metaphor is that the shepherding journey is never-ending. The journey is like a spiral - cyclic in nature - never returning to the same point - always climbing or descending.

The Shepherd Metaphor

Sensing the spirit

Guiding Principle: *Life is the precious gift*

Shepherd Attributes	Shepherd Values
Integrity	Respect
Trust and Trustworthy	
	Truth
Prophecy	
Transcendence and Faith	Authenticity
Empathy	Resilience
Compassion and Passion	
	Tolerance
Intuition	
Risk	Ingenuity
Judgment	Wisdom
Diversity	
Communication	
Consistency	

Shepherd Actions

Gathering	Presence
Vision and mission	Always there

Pathfinding
Guide for the journey

The following sections will explore the abstract nature of the image of a shepherd to provide a framework for leadership in the context of a moral community. A moral community in which members may strive towards shared principles, values and beliefs. In this sense members of a community can aspire to become leaders assuming different roles at various times (McCormick & Davenport, 2003; McGahey, 2000). A community member may act as a leader, or they may be prepared to follow and be happy to remain as a part of the flock when attending to the flocks needs.

Within the concept of a moral community, one would hope a spirit of good intent would prevail. That is, thoughts and actions would emerge from the goodness of one's heart and, collectively, from the goodness of people's hearts - people would sense the spirit.

The three interconnected features of the Shepherd Metaphor for Leadership are The Guiding Principle, The Leadership Attributes and The Leadership Actions (Gathering, Pathfinding and Always There). These are described in detail below.

A. Guiding Principle

'It is not more light that is needed in the world; it is more warmth. We will not die of darkness but of cold.' (Jenny Read)

The essence of leadership is poignantly expressed in this quote by sculptor Jenny Read in Cooper & Sawaf (1997, p. 215). It is leadership that shines like a beacon to attract people, but also keeps people together through the sheer warmth emanating from the source – the warmth is what will draw people towards the leader. This warmth is expressed through qualities such as empathy and compassion. These attributes arise from the principles and values that profoundly influence human thoughts and deeds (Covey, 1994; Goleman, 1997; McGahey, 1997; Sergiovanni, 1992, 1994; Starratt, 1994). Stephen Covey believes there is a clear distinction between a principle and a value:

'Principles are not values. A gang of thieves can share values, but they are in violation of the fundamental principles we are talking about. Principles are, the territory. Values are the maps. When we value correct principles, we have truth -a knowledge of things as they are.' (Covey (1994, p. 35)

Within the model, there is only one principle: Life is the precious gift. The critical word here is 'life'. It is life that is the gift – each breath we take. The gift is not the possessions one acquires in life. Being alive and living is the gift.

'Life is the precious gift' is the foundation upon which the model rests. There is no better story than the biblical parable of The Lost Sheep (Luke 15: 3–6). The shepherd leaves the 99 sheep to go and search for the one lost sheep. He knew the flock could look after itself while he ventured to find the lost one. The importance of the individual above the needs of the collective resonates here. The parables of the Prodigal Son (Luke 15: 11–32) and the Good Samaritan (Luke 10: 30–37) also follow this theme.

Several human values and likely behaviours reflect this principle. These are derived from the work of several writers, including Bezzina (2012), Covey (1994), Dreher (1997), Fullan (1988), McGahey (1993), Sergiovanni (1992, 1994) and Wenniger (1997). Most of these values have been iterated in the works of Greenleaf (1977) and others who speak of servant leadership (Gardner, 1990; Shelton, 1997; Spears, 1995; Starratt, 2005, 2012). The following list is not inclusive of all possible values, but most are linked to those listed below. Each value is given a description of it's meaning:

- **Respect** – for human life and the dignity of every person.
- **Truth** – seek the truth. Without truth, there is no trust and no hope.
- **Authenticity** – what you see is what you get.
- **Resilience** – acknowledge the situation without allowing it to destroy you within.
- **Tolerance** – an acceptance of the things you can change and those you cannot.
- **Ingenuity** – make something out of nothing; seek to create.
- **Wisdom** – listen to the voice within. This voice is your best teacher to build and create a future filled with goodness.

Each of the values can be fostered in practices that reflect the attributes and actions of a leader as given in The Shepherd Metaphor. In this way, authentic relationships of trust are built and nurtured. As previously stated, several writers in the field of leadership have realised the significance of relationships (personal and group) in organisations and the formation of communities (Bezzina, 2012; Bowling, 2011; McGahey, 2000[b]; Sergiovanni, 1996; Starratt, 2012.

From these values, several attributes arise that give purpose to the leader's role. These attributes are considered essential for the leader within the context of a moral community – a community in which every member endeavours to live as leaders who lead with grace.

B. Leadership Attributes - aspiring to lead with grace.

An essential feature of the metaphor are the attributes that a leader should search to find within themselves. These attributes are a gift given to all. In other words, we can aspire to live by them in our daily lives. We need the situation(s) that allow us to display them. The 15 attributes used in a study that explored leaders' beliefs and philosophies in the formation of a moral community within the context of a Catholic school (McGahey, 2002). Many of these attributes have evolved from the previous work of the author (McGahey, 1993; 1997; 2000; 2002). The study concluded there were six key attributes leaders needed to develop within themselves as they strived to build community. Subsequent work has aligned the other attributes under the six key attributes. The following list presents the attributes of a leader.

1. *Integrity*
   - *Trustworthy*
   - *Willingness to Trust*
2. *Prophecy*
   - *Transcendence*
   - *Faithfulness*
3. *Empathy*
   - *Compassion*
   - *Passion*
4. *Intuition*
   - *Risks.*
5. *Judgement*
   - *Diversity*
6. *Communicate*
   - *Consistency*

These attributes have evolved from literature research and subsequent literature reviews in a Masters dissertation (1993) and a Doctorate thesis (2001) by this author. The areas of study included human resources management, leadership, moral community, teaching and learning. A reference list is given at the end of this appendix.

Since that time, the leadership attributes have been further developed and used in several models to describe the attributes required of a person, whether as a leader and/or as a follower. These attributes are what people should aspire to develop within themselves and bring to life through their action(s).

The following describes the 15 attributes. The study and subsequent analysis revealed the connections between each attribute. The six key attributes and their associated satellite attributes appear in the book _Leadership Attributes for Men and Women: Leading Community in Disruptive Times._

Appendix B displays a shortened description of the Leadership Attributes.

1. Integrity

'Like leadership itself, integrity is something you are, not something you do.' (Bowling, 2011, p. 19)

The Macquarie Dictionary defines integrity as 'the condition of being whole; honest' (Bernard, 1989). A study of more than 10 years duration with 15,000 managers worldwide, discovered that integrity was the attribute most looked for in a leader (Dreher, 1997, p.270).

This finding is supported by the results

of a study that explored the perceptions, thoughts and feelings of school leaders who are actively engaged in the establishment of schools as moral communities (McGahey, 2002). Every participant had placed integrity as one of the five most significant attributes required for establishing a moral community from of a possible twelve to fifteen attributes. Further statistical analysis revealed they had ranked integrity as 1 or 2 in the ranking.

However, how is integrity found and nurtured?

The shepherd carried very little while grazing the flock and would spend many hours alone, sitting and watching. Integrity is found in the quiet recesses of the heart and soul. It is nurtured by the time one spends reflecting upon personal principles and values and how these are expressed in the living of life.

Honesty builds integrity which, in turn, creates trust. Shepherd leaders need to practise openness and see themselves as being worthy of a community's trust - being trustworthy.

In short…
Integrity is being whole as the person you

are; honest with yourself. Integrity is found in the quiet recesses of the heart and soul. It is nurtured by the time one spends reflecting upon personal principles and values and how these are best expressed in the living of life.

Trust

To become trustworthy you must be willing to trust. Those who do not show a willingness to trust others cannot expect to be trusted. A leader should be the first to offer the hand in trust. Trust can be seen as the highest form of human motivation that brings out the best in people (Covey, 1994, p.178). The shepherd and the flock would have embedded a great deal of trust in each other (Carnes, 2007; McCormick & Davenport, 2004).

Ultimately, the best in people is what is needed to encourage authenticity and lasting relationships built upon the foundations of trust.

In short…
To trust is to take a leap of faith. It is the willingness to trust that is essential. If you do not show a willingness to trust, how can you expect to be trusted?

Trustworthy

To be worthy of another's trusted you must first show that you trust them. Trustworthiness is a two-way street.

A shepherd would gain the flock's trust through clear communication and by providing food. The shepherd leader will need to communicate openly with others so as to be worthy of another person's trust. Within the community the led need to believe that the leader will make judgements based upon competence and values rather than self-interest (Bowling, 2011; Sergiovanni,1992).

The leader should make explicit their personal principles and values to others. Within a moral community, this should be done continuously with passion and sincerity.

In short…
To be worthy of another's trusted you must first show that you trust them. Those who do not show a willingness to trust others cannot expect to be trusted. It is a double-edged sword and trust is a two-way street.

2. Prophecy

Leadership will often require a person to be prophetic and challenging when striving to build community. It may require them to be prepared to make a stand should the need arise.

A leader should begin a journey with the end in mind, but not fearful of the outcome. Leaders need to remain self-motivated, confident and ready to articulate their vision (prophecy) of the future for the community.

There are numerous examples of leaders past and present who were considered prophetic and challenging in thoughts and actions - Nelson Mandela, Mahatma Gandhi, Mother Theresa, Mary Mackillop, Jesus of Nazarus, Socrates, Chomsky (philosopher) and Bertrand Russel (philosopher). There are also leaders such as past directors, CEO's, principals, teachers and family members. Leaders should seek to find the greener pastures as did the shepherds of old (Anderson, 1997; Leniak, 2006; McCormick & Devenport, 2004; McGahey, 2000). Moreover, never be too fearful of the challenge that lies ahead-just cautious.

In short...

There is a need for each of us, as individuals, to become prophets of our own future. This will take courage and the willingness to take a stand and to accept the challenge. In a world that experiences suffering and sorrow on a grand scale, now, more than ever, we need to be prophets of hope.

Transcendence

Bennis and Nanus (1985) first described this attribute as a kind of magic with the ability to bring aspects of change, dilemma and ideas together within a single vision of the future that is understandable, desirable and life-giving.

There was one noted period of biblical history when the shepherds of Israel wandered in the desert for forty years (Numbers 32:13). These shepherds, the chosen people, were punished for the sin of pride against God. Nevertheless, they still believed in the future of their nation (community) and in the compassion of God.

Shepherd leaders need to remain self-motivated and ready to articulate their graceful vision of the future. A vision can become "shared" through changes made in open dialogue with other members of the community. In this sense, a shepherd leader will need to be prophetic and challenging.

In short...
Transcendence is our inherent awareness of our place in the world. It is purity and perfection, eminence and excellence, goodness and grace. It is a moment in time when one has a clear vision of the future that is energising and desired.

Faithfulness

A firm belief in a future.

The future of the flock and the hope of a season of good breeding and the fattening of lambs, always saw the shepherd looking ahead to the next feed and place of safe rest.

This shepherd attribute grows with the other 14 attributes as they emerge through the actions of the shepherd leader. Altogether they provide the hope for the future of the moral community.

Fundamentally, faithfulness is the belief in oneself and the principles, values and beliefs one holds dear. The shepherd leader can bring people together through such faith. From this gathering, shared principles, values and beliefs can emerge with a graceful vision for a grace-filled mission of a future that is both energising and desirable.

In short…
Faith is the belief in oneself and the principles, values and beliefs one holds dear. Faith is also a belief in a future. Sometimes that future is not of our own making.

3. Empathy

The art of listening and feeling.

The traditional shepherd would communicate openly with the flock (Anderson, 2013; Laniak, 2006; McCormick & Davenport, 2003; McGahey, 2000). The shepherd would become familiar with the sights and sounds of the flock as they communicated with each other and would take the time to listen - to feel and empathise.

Effective leaders listen empathetically. Shepherd leaders need to increase their empathy by taking the time to listen and immerse themselves in the problems and issues of others. They should show a willingness to communicate openly and honestly. This action would develop trust and believability which displays a person's integrity.

Such feeling and listening will encourage honest dialogue between people and within a community. Hence, this could lead to a growth in integrity within people themselves and the whole community.

In short...
We need to increase our empathy by taking the time to listen and immerse ourselves in the problems and issues of others. To endeavour to stop, cut off the chatter in our heads, and really feel for others.

Compassionate

'To be a shepherd leader requires a bold living out of mercy and compassion.' (McCormick & Davenport, 2003, p.29)

Compassion and courage go hand in hand. It takes great courage to be compassionate. It is far easier to destroy an enemy rather than be compassionate toward them. Being compassionate requires trust in oneself, one's own judgement and wisdom. Compassionate action requires stopping, and being willing to seek first to understand; then be understood (Covey, 1994). A shepherd leader shows they care (Kouzes & Posner, 2007, p. 324).

Traditional stories reveal the shepherd to be loving, caring, trustworthy, patient and a tenderness that would see:

'No lamb so tiny that he will not carry it, no saint so weak that he will not gently lead, no soul so faint that he will not give it rest.' (Roper, 1995)

This passage reveals a compassionate and passionate heart with a quiet strength that is reassuringly persistent. Note the word 'passion' within the word 'compassion.' You cannot have one without the other. To be passionate opens a door for compassion; To be compassionate is knowing of the feelings of passion.

In short…
Compassion and courage go hand in hand. Compassion is often regarded as a sign of weakness, but, in fact, it takes great courage to be compassionate – to care and be patient. Compassion requires trust in oneself – in one's own intuitive judgment and wisdom. The act of compassion requires one to give of themselves and to shut out the endless chatter in their head.

Passion

Passion with persistence - enthusiasm that flows from the heart.

A shepherd's passionate love for the land and love for the flock is revealed in the traditional stories, fables and pictures of the shepherd. Traditional images of a shepherd show the shepherd carrying a lamb in one hand, or across the shoulders and, in the other hand a crook (walking stick). The clothing was practical and befitting the rugged outdoor lifestyle led by a shepherd.

The need for leaders to be close to and passionate about nature is mirrored in other religions, particularly in Eastern teachings. For example, Buddhism and the Tao Te Ching written by Lao Tzu (Taoism) have many references to leaders, passion, the heart and nature.

'Tao leaders live close to nature.
Their actions flow from the heart.
In words they are true;
In decisions, just.'   (Tao, 8)
(Dreher, 1997, p.218)

The leader can use this attribute to motivate others towards actions that will create and sustain a sense of community - a sense of belonging. To lead with grace requires the shepherd leader to create the environment were authentic and trusting relationships thrive.

The leader should always be passionate towards seeking the truth by being enthusiastic about that which they feel is good and true. In other words, the shepherd leader should use intuition (feeling for the truth).

In short...
Passion is enthusiasm and persistence that flows from the heart. We can use this attribute to motivate people towards actions that will create and sustain a sense of community—a sense of belonging.

4. Intuition

The Macquarie Dictionary defines intuition as "the direct perception of truth" (Bernard, 1989). The inner voice - human intuition has long been regarded as one of the best tools for finding solutions to questions of purpose (life, personal, community direction). Einstein, Plato and Jung spoke of intuition as an essential feature of an individual's thinking. All used their intuition to help inspire them to make many significant contributions to benefit humankind. Einstein once stated:

'I believe in intuition and inspiration...at times I feel certain I am right while not knowing the reason... Imagination is more important than knowledge. For knowledge is limited, whereas imagination embraces the entire world, stimulating progress, giving birth to evolution.' (Wagmeister and Shifrin, 2000, p. 48)

Mozart spoke of not knowing were his compositions came from and for Rene Descartes, the ideas on rational thinking came from a dream. (Shelton, 1997, p. 7).

The work of people like Schon (1984) on reflective practice has legitimised the use of intuition and sensing (using the 5/6 senses) in organisational decision making. Schon (1984) believes in reflection in action that allows for instant critique and an intuitive understanding of experience.

The leader needs to look within and be guided by their intuition and should always be compassionate (caring/patient) when revealing the truth.

In short...
Intuition is said to be an unconscious form

of knowledge that rests just below the conscious level of thought. It is an inner voice – the direct perception of truth. The inner voice has long been one of the best tools for finding solutions to questions of purpose (life, personal and community direction).

Risk

Biblical stories such as the parable of The Lost Sheep (Luke15: 5-6) reveal the shepherd to be a risk taker. The shepherd left the flock to search the wilderness for the lost lamb. The Good Shepherd had faith in the flock knowing that the flock could be left to fend for itself, even for a short time. This belief freed the shepherd to use his intuition in detecting the loss and then in finding the lost lamb.

Fear of the outcome of an action is the reason why people fear to take risks. It was Gandhi who believed that we should not worry about the outcome of our actions when the action is in line with our principles and values. As stated earlier, he believed that we are not responsible for the outcome. If our motives are true and remain consistent with our beliefs, then we must act and let God do the rest (Dreher, 1997, p. 205).

The leader needs to be willing to trust in themselves and others for risk-taking to be done without fear.

In short...

Fear of the outcome of an action is the reason people are afraid to take risks. We should not worry about the outcome of our actions when the action is in line with our principles and values. It was Gandhi who believed that we are not responsible for the outcome. Our duty is to make sure that our motives are pure and our means are consistent with our beliefs. If we take care of our motives and means, the rest will follow naturally.

5. Judgement

The willingness to suspend judgement, exercise detachment from a situation and practising reflection while viewing from different points of view (multiple perspectives) is an essential attribute for building community.

The shepherd is a symbol of wisdom - all knowing. Such wisdom is gained through experience and quiet reflection upon experience. While the flock grazed, the shepherd would reflect and plan the course for night shelter and the following day's journey.

Suspending judgement requires detachment and reflection time:
'The best leader does not use force...The best managers seek to understand their people. This is the practice of detachment. Which brings the power to lead others. Moreover, is the highest lesson under heaven.' (Tao, 68) (Dreher 1997, p. 208)

Through detachment, the leader can call upon their thoughts and feelings through reflective practice to recall the principles, values and other attributes that are needed to make a good decision (McGahey 1997, p.7). John Dewey (1933) believed that we learn more from past reflection upon a learning experience than the actual experience itself. Daniel Golman (1996) speaks of suspending judgement and empathy as key components of emotional intelligence. Therefore, the leader should give themselves and others the 'gift of time' to reveal the wisdom of the experience. When detachment and suspension of judgement become custom and practice, a leader can listen to all points of view without the need to judge (at least straight away). This attribute also allows for the redemptive side of community life to prevail. We are all in need of forgiveness from time to time.

In other words, the insight gained through reflection on our experiences from multiple perspectives can only occur through detachment and time. Taking time to listen to one's heart and soul (personal principles and values) for the answers to problems is a desirable attribute for a leader. It is this attribute that provides the foundation upon which to build a belief in a future - a faith born of personal principles and values.

In short…

The willingness to suspend judgment and to practise reflection while considering from different points of view is essential (multiple perspectives). Being able to suspend judgment requires detachment and reflection time. We do not actually learn from experience as much as we learn from reflecting on that experience.

Diversity

Diversity is a strength in community - the capacity to solve problems is greatly enhanced through different minds.

'Unity through diversity; diversity in unity.'

One of the participants of the study indicated that diversity as an under-utilized strength (McGahey, 2002). Leaders are encouraged to build leadership teams that have people who display different talents, gifts, skills and knowledge. Indeed, it is through continuous dialogue that acknowledges and promotes diversity of opinion to be shared that new 'synergetic' realities are being born.

A leader will seek diversity and create the environment where diversity is accepted and encouraged as a means of signalling the possibility of change. The shepherd could not keep going back to regular feeding grounds as the flock grew, newer ground needed to be found. The wise shepherd also allowed the flock to interbreed. Hence, a healthy variety and diversity within the gene pool. There was less likelihood of genetic diseases and disorders.

In short…
Diversity is a strength! Our different traits and personalities can be used as strengths to build community. Our diversity is our uniqueness. Diversity is what creates opportunity. Diversity within unity: unity through diversity.

6. Communication

The willingness to communicate and empathy are linked (the art of listening and feeling).

As previously stated, a good shepherd would communicate openly with the flock. (Anderson, 2013; Laniak, 2006; McCormick and Davenport, 2003; McGahey, 2000). The shepherd would develop and train the flock in the use of signals and sounds. These sounds would warn the flock of danger, and the need to regroup or split up. In the morning each shepherd who gathers his flock through a distinctive guttural sound and lead them to their own feeding grounds (Anderson 1977; Roper 1995). The shepherd would become familiar with the sights and sounds of the flock as they communicated with each other. The shepherd would take the time to listen.

To really listen requires the ability to shut off the chatter in one's head as you listen to another speak. This ability takes time to master and is an essential leadership skill.

A leader will need to communicate openly with people through whatever medium is thought to be best (voice, written and action). Leaders often fail to communicate through lack of knowledge or skill, but if there is the will or intent to communicate, then one can assume that some action will be taken to rectify a problem. The leader should always be willing to develop and open lines of communication. The same willingness should be evident in the taking of risks, in trust and in suspending judgement.

In short…
We need to communicate openly with people through whatever medium is thought to be best (voice, written, action). Take the time to listen. We often fail to communicate through a lack of knowledge or skill, but if there is the will or intent to communicate, then one can assume that some action will be taken.

Consistency

A leader should strive to be consistent in all things. Therefore, treat others equitably including oneself.

Consistency is a sense that others have about a leader who is 'always there.' A leader who is always there to offer support and guidance to those in need. Consistency within this context does not mean doing everything the same every time. It means being consistent in your treatment of people and their perceived needs.

A shepherd was always attending to the needs of the flock. They knew each sheep by name (John 10: 27) and would tend to their individual needs. In this way treated them as equals.

In short...
Within this context, consistency does not mean doing everything the same way every time. It means being consistent in one's treatment of people. Consistency is a sense that someone is 'always there'. People are quick to ascertain if a person is someone who is always there to offer support and guidance to all.

The attributes should not be seen as definite attributes that require a "more than human" person to live them. They are ideals that everyone can strive to find within themselves and then through their activities as they move themselves and others towards greener pastures.

The attributes of a leader transcend every aspect of the Shepherd Metaphor to reach into the soul of organisational leadership work. These attributes should be made explicit as they are the substance, strength and motivation behind every Shepherd Actions.

The attributes, founded through a shared principle and shared values and beliefs, should emerge from within the hearts, souls and minds of the members of a moral community. The shepherd actions can then evolve through the active participation of the community to live fully a shared graceful vision for a grace-filled mission. Therefore, a community should not need to overreact to challenge and change. As Bowling (2011, p. 41) states 'change is not the enemy; changing the wrong things is. It takes grace to know the difference.'

The actions of a leader should emerge and flow from the graceful vision for a grace-filled mission. The following section will detail the role of the leader while incorporating the attributes of a leader.

C. Leadership Actions - The Role of the Leader

The leader is the guardian of the vision and mission (their own and a shared vision and mission of the community). The actions and roles they play need to eliminate from the vision and mission. As previously stated, within the concept of leading with grace the vision and mission can be thought of as:

'A graceful vision for a grace-filled mission is a call to action.'

The guiding principle, associated values and leadership attribute once acknowledged and articulated by a leader sets the scene for a graceful vision and grace-filled mission. This will lead to action which can in the service of others.

The role of a leader can be thought of as areas of action such as:

Gathering - vision and mission
Pathfinder - guiding
Always There - never alone

The strength of each area of action is dependent upon the explicitness and predominance of the Guiding Principle and the Leadership Attributes within a community. The attributes should be evident in the three actions. However, at times, certain attributes will be more evident than others. The following sections will describe the three actions in light of leadership and the attributes of a leader. In this way, the graceful vision for a grace-filled mission becomes a call to action in the service of others.

Gathering - vision & mission

'The Tao leader creates harmony
Reaching
From the heart
To build community.' (Toa, 49)
(Dreher, 1997, p.246)

The gathering action - is what leads to the formation of a community. A leader's vision, mission and plan are tools that can be used to gather people and gain the support needed for the establishment of a moral community. A shepherd leader would use their vision and mission to inspire others to gather (Kouzes & Posner, 2007, p. 141). When shepherd leaders' actions reflect the attributes of a shepherd, a sense of unity, respect and belonging will prevail. This belonging will eventually lead to the gathering - a gathering of collective minds every one different and unique.

Through shared dialogue, a single vision and mission can grow into a shared vision and mission. In this way, the gathering/community creates a shared graceful vision for a grace-filled mission which is a call to action. People will be united through a shared purpose based on shared principles, values and attributes.

The actual role of being a leader can be assumed at different times by different members of a community. Different circumstances can often require a different mindset and skills. Indeed, every member of the community should aspire to be leaders. In this sense, the gathering is not just left up to the designated leaders, for it can become a shared endeavour amongst every member of the flock.

Once gathered - the flock needs to be directed and guided towards green pastures and a safe resting place. Leaders will become the pathfinders.

Pathfinder - the guide to greener pastures

'Leaders must have the courage to follow their vision (shared), to believe in the invisible, to work for something that is still only a possibility, while others often wring their hands in despair.' (Dreher, 1997, p.138)

Shepherds will seek new paths and new directions in which the vision and mission can flourish and be transformed into action.

They are pathfinders (McGahey, 2000; Bowling, 2011).

As stated several times, a graceful vision for a grace-filled mission is a call to action. To act upon a shared vision and mission requires the use of emotional intelligence and development of intrapersonal and interpersonal skills (Bowling, 2011; Golman, 1996, 1998; Gardener, 1993).

Such action can create a steep learning curve in people who will involve the use of power and emotion (Glickman 1986, Calhoun 1985, Hunt and Joyce, 1967). This emotion can be harvested and used wisely. For as Goldman (1996, p. 34) states:

'Being able to motivate oneself and persist in the face of frustrations; to control impulse and delay gratification; to regulate one's moods and keep distress from swamping the ability to think; to empathise and to hope.'

These abilities take time to develop within a person. They require a degree of self-awareness, authenticity, transparency, resilience, empathy with others perspectives, tolerance, acceptance of differences and the will to seek to build authentic grace-filled and trusting relationships. To be a pathfinder a person needs to be willing to adopt actions that display flexibility, adaptability, openness to new ideas and practices, accountability, ingenuity and innovativeness (Bredfeldt, 2006; Gow, 1997; Lowney, 2003). These can be fostered and nurtured through the attributes and actions as given in the Shepherd Leadership Metaphor.

The leader as Pathfinder will need to find within themselves the attributes of passion, faith (a belief in a bright value led future) and transcendence (Bowling, 2011; Bredfeldt, 2006; Lowney, 2003; McGahey, 2001, 2002). This will need to be a cornerstone and the foundation upon which a moral community is built. The pathfinders will need to be willing to trust the community in shared decision making.

Leadership comes from within, it is a knowing, a calling that speaks of goodwill and prosperity through the sharing of insight and truth. It can be found in one's intuition. It is leadership that has people as the most valuable resource. Therefore, leadership can be a shared reality (Carnes, 2006; McCormick & Davenport, 2003). Once again, different members of a community may step forward to be the leader depending on the terrain ahead. Leadership needs to be dynamic as the context, task and followers need a change from event to event and situation to situation. As the author has on previous occasions has stated:

'The shepherd is spiritual, a wanderer of open spaces, freedom and greener pastures. The shepherd will mingle with the flock walking sometimes behind, sometimes in front but usually within the flock.' McGahey (2000, 2001)

And as Loa Tzu taught, leaders are able to:

'Live with humility, Remaining ahead of their people, By walking behind.' (Toa, 66) Dreher (1997, p. 231)

Just as the Good Shepherd is always there, within a moral community, leaders should always be there to listen, lead, mingle within, or at times only follow. This raises a vital task for leaders to consider, reflect on and act upon - succession planning. There is a serious neglect of this leadership act within our world today. The horrific events of war that still persist in our world and the economic crisis are a testament to this.

Succession needs to be planned,

managed and people need to be taught and nurtured to take on leadership responsibilities depending on the gifts they bring to community. It needs to be ongoing with the net being cast out many times as given in the Bible (The Apostle St Peter known as 'the fisher of men'). Succession should never be narrowed down or limited to 'the one'. Different situations and terrain require different skill sets, mindsets, capabilities, capacities and abilities.

Communities and organisations should not be monarchies or dictatorships. Bad choices are made when succession planning means the hunt is on for the one or the few and is left too late - as the ship sinks. Succession planning should begin on day one of the start of any new leadership role or job. Likely candidates can be mentored, coached and nurtured for future leadership possibilities.

Therefore, leaders need to be always searching with passion, always seeing ahead and being guided by their intuitive heart and soul, always believing in a bright future (Attributes). Pathfinding will require some risk-taking and leaders will need to become trailblazers who are living examples of the competencies and skills to be lived and taught.

A shepherd is a guide to greener pastures of tranquillity, satisfaction, protection and rest. (Anderson, 1997; Leniak, 2006; McCormick & Devenport, 2004; McGahey, 2000). Shepherd Leaders will need to evoke a vision for their community that includes a shared oasis with quiet peaceful waters to drink and bathe at the end of a long hard trail.

Always There (theme) - presence

'A good shepherd never left his sheep alone.
   They would have been lost without him.
   His presence was their assurance.'
   (Roper, 1997, p.3)

The Tao Te Ching as translated by Dreher (1997, p.131) discloses:

'Without the One, the heavens would fall,
   The earth would die,
   The spirits would mourn,
   The valleys dry up.' (Toa, 39)

This action - Always There - is vital for developing endurance and perseverance amongst the flock and therefore within community. The leader's presence should always be felt through their actions.

Leaders must be seen as "trustworthy, fair and consistent. There is a need for leaders to be willing to communicate openly and become:

'The constant voice that calls for ethical commitment, vision, behaviour, achievement and courage...someone must be the keeper of the corporate conscience. Someone must remind the organisation of the need to err on the side of goodness.' (Larimer, 1997, p.5)

The shepherd knows the sheep by name and knows every cut and bruise they carry (empathy). Leaders should display compassion and caring that is open to those in need. Through a leader's actions, a leader's integrity shines forth.

During the day a shepherd would stay close to his sheep, observing them while feeding and protecting them from the slightest harm (Anderson, 1997; Carnes, 2006; Laniak, 2006). If one sheep strayed, the shepherd searched for it until it was found. At night each shepherd led his flock to the safety of the fold and slept across the gateway to protect them (Roper, 1997).

D. To Lead with Grace - a venture into the soul

Thus far we have seen...

The Shepherd Metaphor for Leadership is a metaphor for establishing relationships that build community. At the heart of the metaphor is the development of a shared graceful vision for a grace-filled mission which is a call to action. This shared vision and missions strength is forged from a common set of values that unite a community (Bowling, 2011, p. 21). The shepherds of old realised that their food, their clothing and family honour was secured by the way in which they cared after their flock (Anderson, 1997, p. 2).

To lead with grace a leader will 'coach rather than control, mentor as well as manage, strengthen others, not only supervise their work, empower, not just employ' (Bowling, 2011, p. 20). It is leadership that focuses on spirit rather than style or means. However, to define spiritual growth and measure it remains a difficult and relatively un-researched paradigm (Cormode, 2002, p. 82).

To lead with grace, requires a venture into ones soul (Bolman & Deal, 2011; Bowling, 2011; Greenfield and Ribbins 1993; Shelton 1997; McCormick & Davenport, 2003; Starratt 1993a; 1993b; 1994; 1996; Wenniger 1997a; 1997b; Westerhof 1997). Taking the time to stop and listen to the still small voice within (Lowney, 2009, p. 145). For many, the small voice is essentially a spiritual experience (Lowney, 2003, p. 19) and this can be a blending of spirit and truth (Bredfeldt, 2006, p. 153). Though many would claim there is no empirical evidence for the existence of a soul it is still a concept a little difficult to dismiss.

As the Barna Group survey (2003) revealed 8 out of 10 people in America do believe in a human soul and an afterlife (McCormick, 2004, p. 3).

This venture into ones soul is a discovery of self and the giving of gifts such as the gifts of love, the gifts of authorship (freeing the intelligence), and the gifts of significance (celebration of rituals, stories and ceremonies). The journey is not without risk. It will take courage to accept our imperfections and to be vulnerable (Wenniger (1997b, p.8). But there is much to be gained through authentic relationships that reside within community. There is a need for valuing the heart, soul and mind of people as well as developing and nurturing their gifts and talents (Bowling, 2011, p. 37), Lowney (2009, p. 151) and McCormick (2003, p. 25). Leadership that values people is a simple concept when aligned to a shepherds' vision and plan. Leadership within community, should reflect the simplicity and soul of a shepherd.

The attributes, founded through a shared principle, values and beliefs should emerge from within the hearts, souls and minds of every member of a moral community. The Leadership Actions can then evolve through the active participation of the community to live a shared graceful vision for a grace-filled mission. Therefore, a community should not need to overact to challenge and change. As Bowling (2011, p. 41) states 'change is not the enemy; changing the wrong things is. It takes grace to know the difference.'

A shepherd-led community would realise that their security is not based on external sources but on an inward principle and associated values and attributes that form a foundation stone for a graceful vision for a grace-filled mission that is a call to action in the service of others – where the actions seem effortless, paradoxical and defying all logic because:

> 'The best runner leaves no tracks ...
> The best door needs nothing to secure it.
> The best knot does not bind,
> Yet cannot be loosened.' (Tao, 27)
> (Dreher, 1997, p. 257)

So our task as leaders is simple – be still and watch; remain mindful and filled with hope, but still willing to make a decision when needed. Indeed, this is grace in its purest form – a graceful vision for a grace-filled mission is a call to action.

Simplistic by design, the Shepherd Metaphor is a path for those who seek to lead with grace. The Shepherd Metaphor is not associated with a set of skills or managerial tasks that can be taught. Indeed, the guiding principle, the leadership attributes and the leadership actions need to be found, developed within and then lived through action–and, not only by those in leadership or who seek leadership roles. The Shepherd Metaphor is a metaphor for living a good life. However, the teachings of the metaphor must first be desired, then sought, found, and lived in our daily life with each breath we take.

Conclusion

To lead with grace…

The two concepts of 'grace'and 'leadership' have been described through the use of a metaphor - 'The Shepherd Metaphor of Leadership.' This metaphor strikes at the heart of what is fundamentally human and humane.

When considered together 'grace and leadership' can lead to a life that is served and a life that gives service while reaching within the soul to reveal what it is to lead with grace - a life of contemplative reflection translated into a vision and a mission which is a call to action…The shepherd Metaphor of Leadership.

And, therefore a path of hope.

'To lead with grace is a path of hope.'

References

ANDERSON, L. (1997). They smell like sheep: Spiritual leadership for the 21st century. Howard Books.

BARRETT, R.S. (1997). Liberating the corporate soul, HR Focus, 74, pp. 16-17.

BENNIS, W. & NANUS, B. (1985). Leader (New York: Harper & Row).

BERNARD, J.R.L. (1989). The pocket macquarie dictionary, (Qld: The Jacaranda Press).

BERRETH, D. & SCHERER, M. (1993). On transmitting values: A conversation with Amitai Etzioni, Educational Leadership, 51(3), pp. 12-15.

BEZZINA, M., BURFORD, C., DUIGNAN, P., & HOTEL, S. W. Fourth International Conference on Catholic Educational Leadership Directions for Catholic Educational Leadership in the 21st Century: The Vision, Challenges and Reality. 29th July-1st August 2007 .COVEY, S. (1994). Seven habits of highly effective people (New York: Simon & Schuster).

BOLMAN, L. G., & DEAL, T. E. (2011). Leading with soul: An uncommon journey of spirit (Vol. 381) (San Francisco: Jossey-Bass).

BOWLING, J. (2011). Grace-full leadership:Understanding the heart of a Christian leader (Kansas City: Beacon Hill Press).

BREDFELDT, G.J. (2006). Great leader, great teacher: Recovering the biblical vision for leadership (Chicago: Moody publishers).

CALHOUN, E.F. (1985). Relationship of teachers' conceptual level to the utilisation of supervisory services and to a description of the classroom instructional improvement. Paper presented at the Annual Meeting of the American Educational Research Association, Illinois, April.

CARNEGIE, D. (1991). How to win friends and influence people. (Sydney: Angus and Robertson).

CARNES, P. G. (2007). Like Sheep Without a Shepherd: The Shepherd Metaphor & Its Primacy for Biblical Leadership (Doctoral dissertation, Reformed Theological Seminary, Virtual

Campus).

COOPER, R. & SAWAF. (1997).
Executive EQ: Emotional Intelligence in
Business (London: Orion Business).

CORMODE, S. (2002), 'Multi-layered
Leadership: The Christian Leader as
Builder, Shepherd, and Gardener' , in
Journal of Religious Leadership (2), 69-104.

DE BONO, E. (1998). Simplicity
(London: Viking).

DEWEY, J. (1933). How we think
(Lexington , MA: DC Heath).

DINHON - HAYNES, G. (1996). Peace
education: Enhancing caring skills and
emotional intelligence in children. (Eric
Document, ED 399489).

DREHER, D. (1997). The tao of personal
leadership: The ancient way to success
(London: Thorsons).

ETZIONI, A. (1993). The spirit of
community rights, responsibility, and the
communitarian agenda (New York:
Crown).

FULLAN, M.G. (1988). Successful school

improvement: The implementation perspective and beyond (Buckingham: Open University Press).

GARDNER, H. (1993). Frames of mind (New York: Basic Books).

GARDINER, P. (1994). Mary MacKillop: An Extraordinary Australian: the Authorised Biography (Sydney:E.J. Dwyer).

GARDNER, J.W. (1990). On leadership (Canada: The Free Press).

GLICKMAN, C, D. (1986). Developing teacher thought. Journal of Staff Development, 7(1), pp. 6-21.

GOLEMAN, D. (1996). Emotional intelligence: Why it can matter more than IQ (London: Bloomsbury).

GOLEMAN, D. (1998).Working with emotional intelligence (London: Bloomsbury).

GOODWIN, D. K. (2009). Team of rivals: The political genius of Abraham Lincoln. ePenguin.

GOW, K. (1997). What are the required outcomes of education- professional competencies, personal attributes and social skills. Paper presented at the Queensland State Conference of National Association of Post Compulsory Educators, Surfers Paradise, Gold Coast, Australia. (Eric Document, ED 407569).

GREENFIELD, T & RIBBINS, P. (1993). Greenfield on educational administration: Towards a humane science (London: Routledge).

HUNT, D.E. & JOYCE, B. R. (1967). Teacher trainee personality and teaching style, American Educational Research Journal, 4, pp. 253-255.

JAGGAR. (1989). In Pinnell, G., & Matlin, M (Ed).Teachers and research: language learning in the classroom. International Reading Association. (ERIC Reproduction Service No. ED 309401).

KILBURG, R.R. (2012). The evolution of executive conscience and the practice of justice.

KILLION, J. & TODNEM, G. (1991).A Process for personal theory building, Educational Leadership Journal, 48 (6), pp. 14 - 16.

KOUZES, JAMES M., AND BARRY Z. POSNER. (2007). The leadership challenge. Vol. 4. (San Franscisco: Jossey-Bass).

LANIAK, T. (2006). Shepherds after My own Heart: Pastoral traditions and leadership in the Bible (Vol. 20). IVP Academic.LANIAK, T. (2006). Shepherds after My own Heart: Pastoral traditions and leadership in the Bible (Vol. 20). IVP Academic.

LARIMER. L. (1997). Reflections on Ethics and integrity, HR Focus, 74, pp. 5.

LEWIS, T., & POTTER, E. (2012). Ethical consumption: a critical introduction. Routledge.

LICKONA. T. (1993). The return of character education, Educational Leadership Journal, 51(3), pp. 6-11.

LUCIA. A. (1997). Leaders know how to listen, HR Focus, 74, pp. 25.

MC DOWELL, J. O. & BELL, E. D. (1997) Emotional intelligence and educational leadership at East Carolina University. Paper presented at the Annual Meeting of National Council for Professors of Educational Administration. (Eric

Document, Ed 414797).

MCCORMICK, B., & DAVENPORT, D. (2004). The Leader as Shepherd. Executive Excellence, 21, 6.

MCCORMICK, B., & DAVENPORT, D. (2003). Shepherd leadership: Wisdom for leaders from Psalm 23 (New York: Jossey-Bass).

MCGAHEY, V.T. (1993). The decisional processes in the establishment of a specialist music school. Unpublished masters dissertation (Edith Cowan University, Perth, WA).

MCGAHEY, V.T. (1997). The most important learners in schools are not the students!, Reflect Journal, 3(1), pp. 6-13.

MCGAHEY, V.T. (2000). Establishing moral community in schools: Sensing the spirit. Unpublished log/diary entries.

MCGAHEY, V. (2000). School leadership for building a moral community: The shepherd metaphor, Leading and Managing, 6(1), pp. 77-94.

MCGAHEY, V.T. (2001). Establishing moral community in schools: Sensing the spirit. Unpublished Doctorate Portfolio.

MCGAHEY, V. (2001). Keeper of the corporate conscience. HR Monthly, March, pp.36-37.

MCGAHEY, V. (2001). Establishing moral community within schools: sensing the spirit. Unpublished doctorate thesis (University of Western Sydney, NSW).

MCGAHEY. V. (2012). Leading With Grace: Sensing the Spirit Within. Paper presented The Australian Council of Educational Leadership International Conference. Brisbane, Australia.

McGAHEY, V. (2013). Leading With Grace: The Shepherd Metaphor for Leadership. Paper presented at the Catholic Leadership Conference. Sydney, Australia.

MICOLO, A. (1996). The human resource survivalist, HR Focus, 73, pp. 19.

MOORE, C., DETERT, J. R., KLEBE TREVIÑO, L. I. N. D. A., BAKER, V. L., & MAYER, D. M. (2012). Why employees do bad things: Moral disengagement and unethical organizational behavior. Personnel Psychology, 65(1), 1-48.

MORRISON, H.B. (1986). Teacher education for moral leadership. Paper presented at the American Educational Studies Association Meeting, Pittsburgh, PA. (Eric Document, ED 278643).

RICHARDSON, R. C. & EVANS, E. T. (1997). Social and emotional competence: Motivating cultural responsive education. Paper presented at the Annual
Conference and Exhibit of the Association for Supervision and Curriculum Development, Baltimore, MD. (Eric Document, ED 411944).

ROPER, D. (1995). The Lord is my Shepherd [online]. Retrieved from

http://www2.gospelcom.net/rbc/ds/hp95 2/hp952/html/ [1999, Nov 10].

RYAN, J. (2017). Commencement Address of 2017. Dean James Ryan of Harvard University [online]. Retrieved from https://www.gse.harvard.edu/news/17/0 5/lead-grace.

RYLATT, A. (1999). Why do our titanic ideas get sunk?, HR Monthly, 6(7), pp. 31-33.

SCHON, D.A. (1984). Leadership as

reflection in action, in T.J. SERGIOVANNI & J.E. CORBALLY (Eds), Leadership and Organisational Culture (Urbana: University of Illinois Press).

SERGIOVANNI, T. (1992) Moral leadership: Getting to the heart of school improvement (San Francisco: Jossey-Bass).

SERGIOVANNI, T. (1994). Building communities in schools (San Francisco: Jossey-Bass).

SERGIOVANNI, T. (1996). Leadership for the school house (San Francisco: Jossey-Bass).

SHELTON, C. (1997). How to use intuition to build a whole-brained organisation,   Women in Higher Education, 6(8), pp. 7.

SPEARS, L. (1995). Reflections on leadership :How Robert K. Greenleaf's theory of Servant leadership influenced today's top management thinkers .

SPICER, A. (2011). Metaphors we lead by: Understanding leadership in the real world. Taylor & Francis.

STARRATT, R.J. (1993a). The drama of

leadership (London: The Falmer Press).

STARRATT, R.J. (1993b). Transforming life in schools (Melbourne: Australian Council for Education Administration).

STARRATT, R.J. (1994). Building an ethical school (London: Falmer Press).

STARRATT, R.J. (1996). Transforming educational administration (New York: McGraw-Hill).

STARRATT, R. J. (2005). Cultivating the moral character of learning and teaching: a neglected dimension of educational leadership. School Leadership and Management, 25(4), 399-411.

STARRATT, R. J. (2012). Cultivating an Ethical School. Routledge.

TAYLOR, D. (1996) The development of human resources for secondary education in Europe: Teaching and non teaching staff - today and tomorrow. Report of the Seminar, Estoril, Portugal for the Council for Cultural Cooperation (Strasbourg, France). (Eric Document, ED 404319).

WAGMEISTER J & SHIFRIN B. (2000). Thinking differently, learning differently,

Educational Leadership, 58(3), pp. 45-48.

WARWICK, J. (1990). Planning human resources development through Equal Opportunity: A hand book. London: Falter Education. (Eric Document ED 332030).

WENNIGER, M. (1997a). Why a president adopts the 'servant leadership philosophy,' Women in Higher Education, 6(8), pp. 2.

WENNIGER, M. (1997b). Learning to lead with soul, Women in Higher Education, 6(7), pp. 8.

WESTERHOF, C. (1997). Let intuition guide your decision making on campus, Women in Higher Education, 6(9), pp. 27.

APPENDIX A: GRACE –
A Brief Historical Account

Grace is a powerful word. However, it can evoke within us a sense of softness and calmness. Grace is seen in action as a form of movement or a simple act - usually one of kindness, graciousness and generosity. The meaning of grace has historical and cultural significance. It is as full of complexity as it is simple.

GRACE

Grace is not seen but is felt.
Often not spoken, but is heard in the silence.
Not always found in some act, but through inaction.
Divine but also human - a gift we can pass onto others.

Grace is all around me as you are at the centre of my thoughts.
It is both a presence and a place.
It is a connection to something bigger than ourselves.

Grace seeks wisdom and wisdom seeks grace.
Grace can be found in a great temple as

well as in a grain of sand.
On the breath of the wind and in the
charism of a good person.

Grace is life-giving, it calls us to serve.
Grace is in the present, past and future
as it will be in the end.
Grace is but a moment in time.

Grace lives within us -
In all of us.

A brief definition of grace from a religious perspective is described below to sense the place of grace within a secular, pluralistic and global world.

'Grace is not defined in words; it is defined in motion and action.' (Casey Kochmer, 2012)

Traditionally grace has been associated with womanhood rather than manhood. To be graceful is a quality usually attributed to a woman. However, modernity has challenged this belief with a 'crossover' and a blending of the sexes where the new age bloke has come of age. Many leaders are finding the grace-filled side of leadership does reap rewards of loyalty, respect and long-lasting relationships that mean you are not alone - you have followers; you have a tribe.

The word grace can mean many things. It is used to describe the attributes (qualities) of a person. Like for example, a disposition to kindness and compassion, and a pleasing or charming quality. A person maybe grace-filled and seen to be gracious. It can be said of such a person 'How gracious you are.' Grace is an ideal that we strive to reach.

The religious and spiritual perspective of grace is of particular significance for many religions. Grace can be used to describe a state of being and a spiritual presence. Grace is said to be a gift from God as given in 1 Peter 5-10: 'God opposes the proud, but gives grace to the humble.' It can be an act of goodwill. The song Amazing Grace stirs the heart and soul of people when played or sung.

The word grace is used to describe an object or a piece of art when expressed as elegance and beauty of movement, form, expression, or proportion. In Greek and Roman mythology grace is associated with three sister goddesses known as Aglaia, Euphrosyne, and Thalia. The sisters dispense charm and beauty to those who sought it

(Kren and Marx, 2012).

(National Galleries, 2012)

The picture depicts the neoclassic sculpture by Antonio Canova (1814 – 1817) of the three sisters. Commissioned by the 6th Duke of Bedford it is displayed in the Victoria and Albert Museum or the National Galleries of Scotland.

It takes time to develop grace in movement, song and any expression of beauty. It requires patience, eloquence and confidence with a dash of quiet humility.

A form of Buddism that began in ancient China is Toaism (4th century). Tao means 'the way' and is often spoken as 'the state of natural grace'. Lau-Tzu is the founder of Taoism and the writer of the Buddhist text 'Tao Te Ching'. Lau-Tzu, gained his insights by observing nature and the state of natural grace. He found that nature has its own way of doing things and we are best to let nature take its course. Hence the idea of 'doing by not doing' which lies at the heart of Taoist philosophy and practice. A simple explanation is the way water naturally flows towards its destination. It will find ways to either seep into, go over or go under any obstacle that lies in its path.

The following is a translation of a portion of Verse 29 of the Tao Te Ching. It has as its theme the notion of doing by not doing:

'Do you think you can take over the universe and improve it? I do not believe it can be done. The universe is sacred. You cannot improve it. If you try to change it, you will ruin it. If you try to hold it, you will lose it. So sometimes things are ahead and sometimes they are behind; Sometimes breathing is hard, sometimes it comes easily; Sometimes there is strength and sometimes weakness. Sometimes one is up and sometimes down. Therefore the sage avoids extremes, excesses, and complacency. (Feng and English, 2012)

So, our task is simple! Be still and watch. This is grace in it's purest form.

Nevertheless, things do need to get done. The critical thing to remember is not to force it. A woodcutter knows it is easier to cut along the grain of the wood then across it. In a constantly changing world, when there has been change after change after change, the fact that there is 'no change' can indeed be a change. This is a poignant lesson for any leader assuming a new role.

The Chinese seem to have grace well defined. Another book called the I Ching has a symbol for grace:

Upper trigram: Kên   *Keeping Still, Mountain*
Lower trigram: Li   *The Clinging, Flame*

The Judgement:

'Grace has success. In small matters. It is favourable to undertake something.'
(Stenudd, 2012)

The symbol represents an image of grace. The image of is that of fire burning at the base of a mountain. The fire is close to the belly of the mountain. It is a warmth that exists even in the biggest giant and is found deep within. What does this symbol represent to us? The mountain is the human body and the fire burning at the base is one's total being - their soul. Its message is found in the judgement as given above:

'Grace has success.
In small matters
It is favourable to undertake something.'
(Stenudd, 2012)

Grace in itself is a call to action.

The Hindu devotional or bhakti literature is full of references to grace as being required for spiritual self-realisation. Some ancient sages taught that the only way to overcome the bondage of living so many lifetimes was through grace. One Hindu philosopher, Madhvacharya, believed that to receive grace you must earn it (Karnataka, 2012).

The teachings of Islam do not entirely reflect Hindu belief. Islam teaches that salvation (paradise) is granted by the grace and mercy of Allah and not just by deeds alone. In other words, to attain salvation, inner belief must be coupled with good works (Hashmi, 2009).

Besides being a short pair of blessing or Thanksgiving said before or after a meal Christian belief teaches us that "grace is a favour, the free and undeserved help that God gives us to respond to his call to become children of God" (Catechism of the Catholic Church, 2000, p. 483). There are

many different forms of grace given to us by
God. Bishop David Walker of the Broken
Bay Diocese introduced the Year of Grace
(2012/13) by describing Sanctifying grace
and Actual Grace. Actual grace is when God
helps in individual situations and
sanctifying grace describes our relationship
to God through the sacrifice of Jesus
(Walker, 2012, p. 3).

According to one source grace is
mentioned 170 times in the Bible (Harrison,
2009). Saint Paul in his letters to the early
Christian communities was a prolific writer
on the topic of grace. The Pauline letters
preached that grace is necessary for
salvation (Romans 3:4; Ephesians 2:8; Titus
2:11; 3:6-7). Titus was one of St Paul's
trusted and known co-workers who wrote
"For the grace of God has appeared,
bringing salvation to all" (Titus 2:11).

St Paul's letters to the early Christian
communities often began with a greeting of
'peace and grace'. Such as in Romans 1:7 'To
all God's beloved in Rome, who are called
to be saints: Grace to you and peace from
God our Father and the Lord Jesus Christ.'

The Catholic Church teaches Christians
that the Holy Spirit is the instrument
through which God gives grace - 'Grace is

first and foremost the gift of the Spirit who justifies and sanctifies us' (Ratzinger, 2000, p. 485). This grace helps us to do the good works which then inspires us to lead with grace. As 2 Corinthians 9: 8-11 reads:

'God is able to provide you with every blessing in abundance, so that by always having enough of everything, you may share abundantly in every good work...you will be enriched in every way for your Great generosity, which will produce thanksgiving to God through us.'

And so to...leading with grace...

The Bible teaches the seven gifts of the Holy Spirit are given to sustain and nourish the moral life of a Christian. These are given in Isaiah 11:1–3 as "wisdom, understanding, counsel, fortitude, knowledge, piety, and fear of the Lord." Saint Paul speaks of the fruits of the Holy Spirit in his letter to the Galatians 5:22–21. These include charity, joy, peace, patience, kindness, goodness, generosity, gentleness, faithfulness, modesty, self-control and chastity. The gifts and fruits are given to help us live a life of service to others and in community.

Jesus beautifully describes what it takes to live a life so these gifts and fruits of the

Holy Spirit can flourish. Wisely in love, faith and hope, Jesus responded through prayer. The prayer is known as the Beatitudes (Matt 5: 1-12). These eight blessed statements are given below. Throughout the ages, many have interpreted and lived by the sentiment of the virtues of grace, gifts and fruits of the spirit.

Matt 5: 1-12

Now when he saw the crowds, he went up on a mountainside and sat down. His disciples came to Him, and He began to teach them, saying:

Blessed are the poor in spirit, for theirs is the kingdom of heaven.

Blessed are those who mourn, for they will be comforted.

Blessed are the meek, for they will inherit the earth.

Blessed are those who hunger and thirst after righteousness, for they will be filled.

Blessed are the merciful, for they shall be shown mercy.

Blessed are the pure in heart, for they will see God.

Blessed are the peacemakers, for they will be called the sons of God.

Blessed are those who are persecuted because of righteousness, for theirs is the kingdom of heaven.

Blessed are you when people insult you, persecute you and falsely say all kinds of evil against you because of me. Rejoice and be glad, because great is your reward in heaven, for in the same way they persecuted the prophets who were before you.

Appendix B: The Leadership Attributes

The following attributes have evolved from literature research and subsequent literature reviews in a Masters dissertation (1993) and a Doctorate thesis (2001) by this author. The areas of study included human resources management, leadership, moral community, teaching and learning. A reference list is at the end of this appendix.

Since that time, the leadership attributes have been further developed and used in several models to describe the attributes required of a person, whether as a leader and/or as a follower. These attributes are what every person should aspire to develop within themselves and bring to life through their action(s).

The 15 attributes are given below. The six key attributes and their associated satellite attributes appear in this book.

1. Integrity

Integrity is being whole as the person you are; honest with yourself. Integrity exists in the quiet recesses of the heart and soul. It is nurtured by the time one spends reflecting upon personal principles and values and how these are expressed in the living of life.

Trust

To trust is to take a leap of faith. It is the willingness to trust that is essential. If you do not show a willingness to trust, how can you expect to be trusted?

Trustworthy

To be worthy of a person's trust you must first show that you trust them. Those who do not show a willingness to trust others cannot expect to be trusted. It is a double-edged sword and trust is a two-way street.

2. Prophecy

There is a need for each of us, as individuals, to become prophets of our future. This will take courage and the willingness to take a stand and to accept the challenge. In a world that experiences suffering and sorrow on a grand scale, now, more than ever, we need to be prophets of hope.

Transcendence

Transcendence is our inherent awareness of our place in the world. It is purity and perfection, eminence and excellence, goodness and grace. It is a moment in time when one has a clear vision of the future that is energising and desired.

Faith

Faith is the belief in oneself and the principles, values and beliefs one holds dear. Faith is also a belief in a future. Sometimes that future is not of our own making.

3. Empathy

We need to increase our empathy by taking the time to listen and immerse ourselves in the problems and issues of others. To endeavour to stop, cut off the chatter in our heads, and really feel for others.

Compassion

Compassion and courage go hand in hand. Compassion can be seen as a sign of weakness, but, in fact, it takes great courage to be compassionate – to care and be patient. Compassion requires trust in oneself – in one's own intuitive judgment and wisdom. The act of compassion requires one to give of themself and to shut out the endless chatter in their head!

Passion

Passion is enthusiasm and persistence that flows from the heart. We can use this attribute to motivate people towards actions that will create and sustain a sense of community – a sense of belonging.

4. Intuition

Intuition is said to be an unconscious form of knowledge that rests just below the conscious level of thought. It is an inner voice – the direct perception of truth. The inner voice has long been regarded as one of the best tools for finding solutions to questions of purpose (life, personal and community direction).

Risk

Fear of the outcome of an action is the reason people are afraid to take risks. We should not worry about the result of our actions when the behaviour is in line with our principles and values. It was Gandhi who believed that we are not responsible for the outcome. We must make sure that our motives are pure and our means are consistent with our beliefs. If we take care of our reasons and methods, the rest will follow naturally.

5. Judgment

The willingness to suspend judgment and to practise reflection while considering from different points of view is essential (multiple perspectives). Being able to suspend judgment requires detachment and reflection time. We do not learn from experience as much as we learn from reflecting on that experience.

Diversity

Diversity is a strength! Our different traits and personalities can be used as strengths to build community. Our diversity is our uniqueness. Diversity is what creates opportunity. Diversity within unity: unity through diversity.

6. Communication

We need to communicate openly with people through whatever medium is thought to be best (voice, written, action). Take the time to listen. We often fail to communicate through a lack of knowledge or skill, but if there is the will or intent to communicate, then one can assume that some action will be taken.

Consistency

Within this context, consistency does not mean doing everything the same way every time. It means being consistent in one's treatment of people. Consistency is a sense that someone is 'always there'. People are quick to ascertain if a person is someone who is always there to offer support and guidance to all.

Bibliography

Bennis, W. & Nanus, B., Leaders: The Strategies for Taking Charge, Harper & Row, New York, 1985, p. 101.

Bezzina, M., 'Paying Attention to Moral Purpose in Leading Learning: Lessons from the Leaders Transforming Learning and Learners Project,' Educational Management Administration & Leadership, 2012:40(2), pp. 248–271.

Bowling, J. C., Grace-Full Leadership: Understanding The Heart of a Christian Leader, Beacon Hill Press, Kansas City, 2011.

Cooper, R. & Sawaf, A., Executive EQ: Emotional Intelligence in Business, Orion Publishing, London, 1997.

Covey, S. R., The 7 Habits of Highly Effective People: Powerful Lessons in Personal Change, Fireside, New York, 1990.

Dewey, J., How We Think: A Restatement of the Relation of Reflective Thinking to the Educative Process, D. C. Heath & Co., Boston, 1933.

Dreher, D., The Tao of Personal Leadership: The Ancient Way to Success, Thorsons, London, 1997.

Fullan, M., What's Worth Fighting For? Working Together for Your School, Ontario Public School Teachers' Federation, Toronto, 1988, pp. 32–36.

Gardner, J. W., On Leadership, Free

Press, New York, 1990.

Goleman, D., Working with Emotional Intelligence, Bloomsbury, London, 1997.

Greenfield, T. & Ribbins, P., Greenfield on Educational Administration: Towards a Humane Science, Routledge, London and New York, 1993.

Greenleaf, R. K., Servant Leadership: A Journey into the Nature of Legitimate Power and Greatness, Paulist Press, Mahwah, New Jersey, 1977.

Greenleaf, R. K., (eds. D. M. Frick and L. C. Spears), On Becoming a Servant Leader: The Private Writings of Robert K. Greenleaf, Jossey-Bass, San Francisco, 1996.

Killion, J. P. & Todnem, G. R., 'A Process for Personal Theory Building,' Educational Leadership, 1991:48(6), pp. 14–16.

Larimer, L. V., 'Reflections on Ethics and Integrity,' HR Focus, 1997:74, p. 5.

Lucia, A., 'Leaders Know How to Listen,' HR Focus, 1997:74, p. 25.

McGahey, V. T., 'Decisional Processes in the Establishment of a Specialist Music School,' unpublished Masters dissertation, Edith Cowan University, Perth, Western Australia, 1993.

McGahey, V. T., 'The Most Important Learners In Schools Are Not The Students!,' REFLECT Journal, 1997:3(1), pp. 6–13.

McGahey, V. T., 'Establishing Moral Community in Schools: Sensing the Spirit –

A Reflective Discourse in Developing an Ethnographic Study and the Subsequent Analysis of Data,' paper presented at the Annual Conference for Doctorate Students, University of Western Sydney, Sydney, Australia, 2000.

McGahey, V. T., 'School Leadership for Establishing a Moral Community: The Shepherd Metaphor,' Leading and Managing Journal, 2000:6(1), pp. 77–94.

McGahey, V. T., 'Establishing Moral Community: Sensing the Spirit,' unpublished doctoral dissertation, University of Western Sydney, Sydney, Australia, 2001.

McGahey, V. T., 'Establishing Moral Community in Schools: Sensing the Spirit of School Leadership,' Leading and Managing Journal, 2002:8(1), pp. 60–77.

Roper, D., 'The Lord is My Shepherd: Rest & Renewal from Psalm 23,' 1995. (Available from Our Daily Bread Ministries at www.ourdailybread.org). Retrieved 10 November 1999, from http://www2.gospel com.net/roc/ds/hp952/html/

Schön, D. A., The Reflective Practitioner: How Professionals Think in Action, Jossey-Bass, San Francisco, 1983.

Schön, D. A., 'Leadership as Reflection-in-Action,' in Sergiovanni, T. J., Moral Leadership: Getting to the Heart of School Improvement, Jossey-Bass, San Francisco,

1992.

Sergiovanni, T. J., Building Community in Schools, Jossey-Bass, San Francisco, 1994.

Sergiovanni, T. J., Leadership for the Schoolhouse: How Is It Different? Why Is It Important?, Jossey-Bass, San Francisco, 1996.

Shelton, C., 'How to Use Intuition to Build a Whole-Brained Organisation,' Women in Higher Education, 1997:6(8), p. 7.

Spears, L. C. (Ed.), Reflections on Leadership: How Robert K. Greenleaf's Theory of Servant-Leadership Influenced Today's Top Management Thinkers, John Wiley & Sons, Inc., New York, 1995, pp. 1–14.

Starratt, R. J., The Drama of Leadership, Falmer Press, London, 1993.

Starratt, R. J., Transforming Life in Schools, Australian Council for Educational Administration, Melbourne, 1993.

Starratt, R. J., Building an Ethical School: A Practical Response to the Moral Crisis in Schools, Falmer Press, London, 1994.

Starratt, R. J., Transforming Educational Administration: Meaning, Community, and Excellence, McGraw-Hill, New York, 1996.

Vines, H., 'The Core of Good Business,' HR Monthly, 1999:6(6), pp. 17–19.

Wagmeister, J. & Shifrin, B., 'Thinking Differently, Learning Differently,' Educational Leadership, 2000:58(3), pp. 45–

48.

Wenniger, M., 'Learning to Lead with Soul,' Women in Higher Education, 1997:6(7), p. 8.

Wenniger, M., 'Why a President Adopts the Servant Leadership Philosophy,' Women in Higher Education, 1997:6(8), pp. 1–2.

Westerhof, C., 'Let Intuition Guide your Decision Making on Campus,' Women in Higher Education, 1997:6(19), p. 27.

FREE POSTER

**Vicky has written a verse on GRACE
which is shared with you in the
opening pages of this book.**

**Get your FREE Copy of selected prose
below…**

Grace is not seen,
but felt

Often not spoken,
but is heard in the
silence

Get My FREE Poster

FREE
hard copy of this BOOK
YOUR FREE link to this PDF OF THIS BOOK

LEAD WITH GRACE:

Leading Community in Disruptive Times
This is the Shepherd Metaphor

NOW AVAILABLE

Get MY Free copy of this book!

FREE WORK BOOK

Get your <u>FREE</u> WORK BOOK to record
your thoughts and reflections.

It includes mandalas to colour in.

The work book is designed to accompany
the book

*<u>Leadership Attributes for Women and Men:
Leading Community in Disruptive Times</u>*

Visit my website for other FREE
resources

<u>www.vickymcgahey.com</u>

Also available at the website is other
helpful resources including **The
Leadership Attributes Game**.

CONTACT EMAIL:
<u>vicky@vickymcgahey.com</u>

Available for Keynote
Presentations and Workshops

NOW AVAILABLE

"THE KINGDOM OF WIZARDS"

Book 1 The Rock and The Rainbow Serpent

Book 2 Abyss (out soon)
Book 3 (draft to editor)

This children's and young adult series features fantasy stories, each founded in reality and filled with mystery and adventure. The stories teach the young mind that the ability to lead lies within us all.

Visit Vicky's website to view her continuing work.